Indian Prairie Library
401 Plainfield Road
Darien, IL 60561

W9-DGN-318

CELEBRATING ALL ABILITIES

BY ABBY COLICH

BLUE OWL
BOOKS

TIPS FOR CAREGIVERS

Social and emotional learning (SEL) helps children manage emotions, learn how to feel empathy, create and achieve goals, and make good decisions. Strong lessons and support in SEL will help children establish positive habits in communication, cooperation, and decision-making. By incorporating SEL in early reading, children will learn the importance of accepting and celebrating all people in their communities.

BEFORE READING

Talk to the reader about abilities. Explain that abilities have to do with someone's capabilities. Discuss that these include physical, mental, and social capabilities.

Discuss: What would you say your abilities are? What is something you are not able to do?

AFTER READING

Talk to the reader about ways he or she can celebrate his or her differences with others.

Discuss: What is one way you can accept another person's ability or disability? Why is it good for a community to be accepting of others?

SEL GOAL

Children may have likely heard to not make fun of or exclude others for being different, but they may not understand why. Talk to readers about the importance of empathy in accepting and celebrating the differences of others. Ask them to imagine what it feels like to be singled out for being different or made fun of for their inabilities. Make a list of these different feelings. Then ask readers to list the feelings they have when they are included and accepted. Explain that our communities are better when everyone is accepted and included.

TABLE OF CONTENTS

CHAPTER 1

WHAT ARE YOUR ABILITIES?

Can you draw comic book characters? Are you a great listener? Maybe you are great at sports. These are your **abilities**! They are the talents or skills you do well.

We all have the ability, or power, to do things. Abilities can look very different. Meg cannot see. That is OK. She knows her abilities. She is a great reader. Everyone is good at something!

Braille

Everyone in your **community** has different abilities. When we celebrate them and work together, we can do so much. Tim's class puts on a play. Tim is a great leader. He directs the play. Carter plays the lead role! Giana is shy. She doesn't like to act. But she loves to paint. She helps make the set!

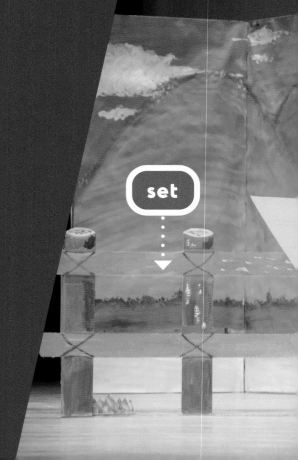

set

CHAPTER 2

RESPECT ALL ABILITIES

When Ethan wins the spelling bee, Mya is jealous. But she tells Ethan, "Good job!" She is a good sport. She respects Ethan and the fact that he won.

Learning and showing **empathy** is a way to show respect. Liam can tell that Mitch is upset. He didn't make the football team. Liam thinks about a time he felt upset and left out, too. He tells Mitch he understands how he feels. He doesn't **brag** about making the team.

Some people have **disabilities**. People with disabilities have awesome abilities, too! Marshon cannot walk, so he uses a wheelchair. He wheels really fast! He practices for races. He has won many of them!

ASK FIRST

You may want to help someone you see with a disability. Always ask first. People with disabilities can often do the same things you can without help.

We can't see some disabilities. Harriet has **ADHD**. She is a great singer! She sings in choir with her class. There is so much more to people than their abilities and disabilities.

GET TO KNOW OTHERS

Talk to someone new. Ask questions about his or her life. Find out what you have in common. Getting to know others will help you understand them. You may see that you are more alike than you thought.

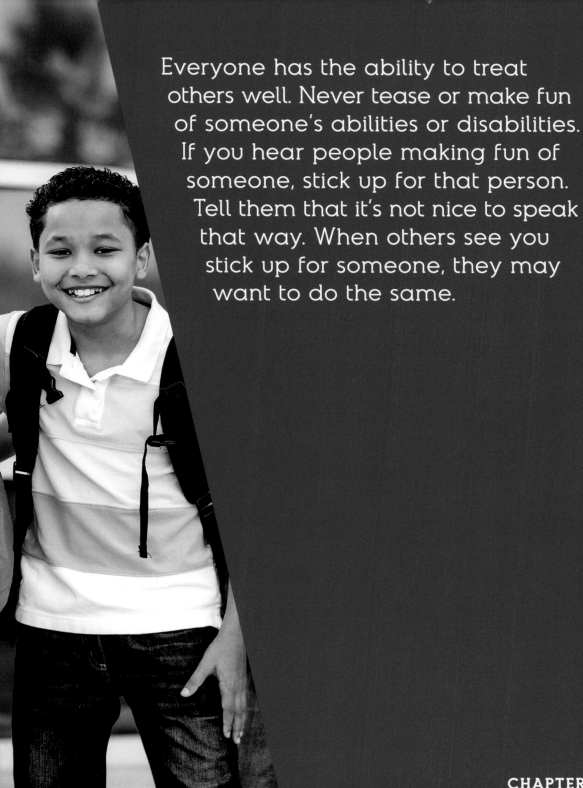

Everyone has the ability to treat others well. Never tease or make fun of someone's abilities or disabilities. If you hear people making fun of someone, stick up for that person. Tell them that it's not nice to speak that way. When others see you stick up for someone, they may want to do the same.

CHAPTER 3

CELEBRATE ALL ABILITIES

We all have abilities. Learn the abilities of those around you. What are your classmates good at? Can you share any of your abilities with them?

Leah is great at spelling. She notices that Sam needs help. Leah quizzes him on his words to help him practice. Then Sam helps Leah with her math homework.

There are many ways to put everyone's abilities to use. For example, everyone on a sports team has different abilities. You work together to play the game. Do you have a group project at school? Use everyone's abilities to finish the task.

When everyone is included, we can all work together. When we work together, we can do so much. What is one way your community can put everyone's abilities to use?

SHARE YOUR ABILITIES

What are you good at? What do you like doing? Write down or draw your abilities. How can you celebrate them and share them with others?

GOALS AND TOOLS

GROW WITH GOALS

Accepting all people, no matter their abilities or disabilities, is important. Focusing on other people's qualities will help you be more accepting.

Goal: Name some things that are more important than a person's abilities. Why should you remember these things when getting to know someone?

Goal: Think of a time you felt empathy toward someone. If you can't think of anything, try to find a time when you can. Do you see someone who looks sad? Ask that person how he or she is feeling and why.

Goal: Get to know someone you haven't spoken with much before. Try to find something you are both good at and enjoy doing.

WRITING REFLECTION

Accepting yourself can help you be more accepting of those around you.

1. What is one thing you are good at or something you like about yourself?

2. What is one thing about yourself you wish you could improve?

3. What is one thing you can do to be more accepting of others?

GLOSSARY

abilities
Skills, or the mental or physical powers to do things.

ADHD
Short for attention deficit hyperactivity disorder; A set of behaviors, including restlessness, too much activity, and difficulty concentrating, that can interfere with learning.

brag
To boast or to talk or act in a certain way to impress others.

community
A group of people who all have something in common.

disabilities
Physical, mental, cognitive, or developmental conditions that can limit a person's ability to do certain tasks.

empathy
The ability to understand and be sensitive to the thoughts and feelings of others.

TO LEARN MORE

FACT SURFER

Finding more information is as easy as 1, 2, 3.

1. Go to www.factsurfer.com

2. Enter "**celebratingallabilities**" into the search box.

3. Choose your cover to see a list of websites.

INDEX

Blue Owl Books are published by Jump!, 5357 Penn Avenue South, Minneapolis, MN 55419, www.jumplibrary.com

Copyright © 2021 Jump! International copyright reserved in all countries. No part of this book may be reproduced in any form without written permission from the publisher.

Library of Congress Cataloging-in-Publication Data

Names: Colich, Abby, author.
Title: Celebrating all abilities / Abby Colich.
Description: Minneapolis: Jump!, Inc., 2021.
Series: Celebrating our communities | Includes index.
Audience: Ages 7–10 | Audience: Grades 2–3
Identifiers: LCCN 2019052392 (print)
LCCN 2019052393 (ebook)
ISBN 9781645273592 (hardcover)
ISBN 9781645273608 (paperback)
ISBN 9781645273615 (ebook)
Subjects: LCSH: Ability—Juvenile literature. | Emotions—Juvenile literature. | Social learning—Juvenile literature.
Classification: LCC BF723.A25 C65 2020 (print) | LCC BF723.A25 (ebook) | DDC 153.9—dc23
LC record available at https://lccn.loc.gov/2019052392
LC ebook record available at https://lccn.loc.gov/2019052393

Editor: Jenna Gleisner
Designer: Michelle Sonnek

Photo Credits: baranozdemir/iStock, cover (left); Patrick Foto/Shutterstock, cover (right); Max Topchii/Shutterstock, 1; Ronnie Chua/Shutterstock, 3; Mark Nazh/Shutterstock, 4; Wavebreak Media ltd/Alamy, 5; Shutterstock, 6–7; Blue Jean Images/Alamy, 8; Motortion Films/Shutterstock, 9; FatCamera/iStock, 10–11; SpeedKingz/Shutterstock, 12–13; kali9/iStock, 14–15; Gelpi/Shutterstock, 16 (left); aldegonde/Shutterstock, 16 (right); Dragon Images/Shutterstock, 17; Konstantin Chagin/Shutterstock, 18–19; SDI Productions/iStock, 20–21; New Africa/Shutterstock, 23 (left); ArtemSh/Shutterstock, 23 (right).

Printed in the United States of America at Corporate Graphics in North Mankato, Minnesota.